FOREVER YOUNG

An Anti-Ageing Guide for the Terrified

Alexandra Filia

Edited by Amy Smylie

ISBN: 978-1-09-147945-6

To every woman fighting the "good" fight and to anyone who has ever gone through the pain of a Brazilian wax. Here's to you!

CONTENTS

Acknowledgements   7

INTRODUCTION   **8**
Vain About Myself, Not My Kitchen   10

WHAT'S HAPPENING TO ME?   **11**
WHAT HAPPENS AT 50?   13
THE FIRST SIGNS   15

MASSIVE CHANGE WITH HIGH EFFORT (CAN HAVE HIGH COST)   **17**
PLASTIC SURGERY   17
    Neck Lift   20
    Breast Augmentation   23
    Tummy Tuck with Liposuction   26
STRENGTH TRAINING   32
    Body Combat and Bingo Wings   32
LASER EYE SURGERY   34
HIFU (HIGH FREQUENCY ULTRASOUND)   36
WARDROBE OVERHAUL   39
    Shopping   41

MASSIVE CHANGE WITH LOW EFFORT AND POSSIBLY LOW COST   **43**
HAIR DYE   43
HAIR EXTENSIONS   45
BOTOX   48
FILLERS   49
PERMANENT MAKEUP   52
NEEDLING   55
EYELASH EXTENSIONS   57
8 MINUTE ABS   59
SKINADE   61
HRT (HORMONE REPLACEMENT THERAPY)   62
ENDOSPHERES   64
TANNING   65
SMILING/TEETH WHITENING   66

MINIMAL CHANGE WITH HIGH EFFORT AND HIGH COST   **69**

THREADING   69
  Neck Threading   70
  Belly Threading   71

MINIMAL CHANGE WITH LOW EFFORT AND POSSIBLY LOW COST   **73**

MANICURE/PEDICURE   73
SUPPLEMENTS   75
COOLSCULPTING (FAT FREEZING)   78
HAIR SERUMS/OLAPLEX   79
FACIALS/GLYCOPEEL   80
CREAMS AND SERUMS   81
LASER TREATMENT   83
  For Discolorations   83
  For Hair Removal   84
MAKEUP AND MAKEUP CLASSES   86

SOME CONSIDERATIONS   **89**
  What if I Don't Have the Money?   89
  I'm Too Afraid of Pain...   90
  My Family/Husband/Kids Do Not Want Me to Change...   92
  I Am in My Late Thirties, Should I Be Doing Anything Now?   93
  I'm Too Busy...   94
  I Don't Want People to Know Because They Will Think That I Am Vain...   94

IN CONCLUSION   **95**
  Is This All There Is?   96
  Rebuilding the Inside   97

ABOUT THE AUTHOR   **99**

Acknowledgements

Dr Spiros Vlachos – Plastic Surgeon. *Athens, Greece*

Victoria Rowse – Personal Trainer. *London*

Dr David Allamby, FRCS (Ed), FRCOphth, Focus Clinic. *London*

Regency Aesthetics. *London*

Moda Donna Beauty Clinic. *Canary Wharf*

Olga Mankovskaia, Permanent Makeup Artist. *London*

Carnaby Laser Clinic & Academy. *Greenwich, London*

Sheena Spencer, Bodytonic Clinic. *Surrey Quays, London*

Makeup London Academy

INTRODUCTION

Nobody warned me that after 22 years of blissful marriage and shortly after my 50th birthday, my significant other and father of my two daughters would bugger off to "find his path to happiness" – presumably in the arms of a less wrinkly version of me. It is, of course, quite surprising that I had not come across this behaviour before…or had I? Casting my mind back to my mom and her middle-aged friends, I now recall this being a rite of passage for men of a certain age. Terrified of death, men seem to want one last hurrah with a pretty little thing. Many, wisely, keep this little indiscretion to themselves. Mine acted on it, and I found myself with two options: either join a nunnery and dedicate myself to God, or pick up the pieces and venture out into the wild west of dating.

I was lucky to land on my feet and in the arms of a fabulous new guy, perfect in every way, except – how shall I put this delicately? – 24 years younger than me. This left me with a problem. Fight the sags and wrinkles, or resign myself to being mistaken for his mother. After some consideration, I chose the former.

Thus started what I like to call the Restoration of the Acropolis. Those of you who have been to Athens and visited the Acropolis may have noticed that it is surrounded by scaffolding. No matter how often you visit Athens, regardless of how many years pass between visits, the scaffolding is always there. For a monument of that age, there is always something to fix.

My journey is now 4 years long. I seem to have knocked about 10-12 years off my appearance. Some of the treatments have been painful, others have been expensive, and not all of them have been worth the pain and suffering. In this book, I will take you through what I have tried and evaluate each procedure based on the pain level, cost and effectiveness.

If you decide to go down this path, you should not turn your back on your real age in terms of your maturity and what it entails. The machinery behind the cosmetic enhancement is still you, with all your experiences, knocks and bruises, successes and triumphs, and that comes with many advantages. I like to think of myself as beautiful and wise: a truly irresistible combination.

It is also a good idea to remember that, no matter what you do, you will not look like a twenty-year-old. Tempting as it is to dress and act like one, or even delude yourself that you look like one, try to stay within the limits of sanity and do not cross over into the ridiculous. It will undo all your good work.

Vain About Myself, Not My Kitchen

Many people spend tens of thousands of pounds remodelling their kitchens and bathrooms. This is perfectly acceptable, and nobody judges them harshly. As for me, I like to spend my money buying time. I prefer to look ten years younger and leave my bathroom and kitchen looking ten years older.

We live in a society that glorifies looking young, yet we have a strong aversion to some body interventions. Spending money and time on fashion, healthy eating, exercise, makeup and hair is not only accepted, but expected. Botox, fillers and plastic surgery are viewed with disdain and attract criticism.

"Embrace your age!" they say. "Age gracefully!" they quip in unison. "Be natural!" ...Really? Where is the line where OK stops being OK according to these self-appointed critics? All of us strive to make our bodies better by dieting, exercising, shaving, going to the dentist, the hairdresser; is this wrong? We all do it every day.

My body, my money, my decision. I expect that many women agree with me, so to those of you I say: read on and get ready to jump into the wonderful world of anti-ageing treatments.

If you are the sort of person that wants to age gracefully, loves their wrinkles because they are life badges, lets their hair go grey and wraps themselves in a comfortable housecoat, you need not read further. Everyone else, read on.

WHAT'S HAPPENING TO ME?

If you are like me, you may have woken up one morning, looked in the mirror and found your mother looking back at you. Sure, there were signs here and there, but the cumulative effect came on quite suddenly.

Having been so busy with life, I did not notice that time was moving on and I had become middle-aged. When I hit 50, as joyous a party as I had, it was a watershed moment. It did not help that my very best friend (a super cute 38-year-old guy) handed me some book about a 50-year-old goddess (with a VERY OLD lady on the cover) as a birthday present. Every day, something new appeared and none of it was welcome. Everything was falling or wrinkling, and that was just the outside. I was tired, lacked energy, wasn't sleeping particularly well, I had hot flushes, my knees were aching and my blood pressure was through the roof.

Thinking of my mom, she always seemed to have the energy of a ping pong ball. Why was I feeling so tired and listless? What did the future hold? Another 30

11

years of steady and relentless decline? Could I do anything about it?

WHAT HAPPENS AT 50?

I have been examining women who have hit the half-century mark, and there are three categories: those who have given up and turned into grandmothers; those who pretend to be in their early twenties and look ridiculous; and the few who look stunning for their age.

This book was written to help you get into this third category. Of course, my experiences are personal to me and my body but much of what I have to say is applicable to everyone, limited only by your budget, perseverance and pain tolerance.

Here are the most common half-century badges that you can look forward to:

➢ Saggy neck – Needs plastic surgery

➢ Saggy boobs – Needs plastic surgery

➢ Limp, thinning hair – Treatments, grow it out, hair extensions

➢ Yellowing teeth – Cosmetic dentist

➢ Wrinkles – Botox

➢ More wrinkles – Fillers

➢ Grandma wardrobe – Overhaul

➢ Bingo wings – Exercise

➢ Love handles – CoolSculpting

➢ Mummy tummy – Tummy tuck

➢ Hormonal imbalance – HRT (Hormone Replacement Therapy)

➢ Plunging energy levels – Supplements

- ➢ Weight in all the wrong places – Diet and exercise
- ➢ Failing eyesight – Surgery
- ➢ Age spots – IPL (Intense Pulsed Light) or laser therapy

THE FIRST SIGNS

There are four broad categories of intervention:

Massive change with high effort (can have high cost)

- *Plastic surgery*
- *Strength training*
- *Laser Eye Surgery*
- *HIFU (High Frequency Ultrasound)*
- *Wardrobe overhaul*

Massive change with low effort and possibly low cost

- *Hair dye*
- *Hair extensions*
- *Botox*
- *Fillers*
- *Permanent makeup*
- *Needling*
- *Eyelash extensions*
- *8 Minute Abs*
- *Skinade*
- *HRT (Hormone Replacement Therapy)*
- *Endospheres*
- *Tanning*

- *Smiling/teeth whitening*

Minimal change with high effort and high cost

- *Threading*

Minimal change with low effort and possibly low cost

- *Manicure/pedicure*
- *Supplements*
- *CoolSculpting (Fat Freezing)*
- *Hair serums/Olaplex*
- *Facials/Glycopeel*
- *Creams and serums*
- *Laser for discolorations*
- *Laser hair removal*
- *Makeup and makeup classes*

MASSIVE CHANGE WITH MASSIVE EFFORT (CAN HAVE HIGH COST)

PLASTIC SURGERY

I will start with the most invasive and expensive intervention, simply because I would like to save you a lot of money on other procedures that claim to be effective and non-invasive. I did try a few and for the areas that bothered me, they simply didn't work. Not at all.

Admittedly, I was a bit nervous about going under the knife, and you should be too. A healthy dose of fear will prevent you from signing up with the first clinic that is willing to take your credit card in the UK or abroad. Do your research and evaluate everything else in addition to the cost. For example:

> ➢ Are you healthy enough for surgery? If you have any health concerns, it's better to hold off. No point in compromising your health or risking your life to have better boobs.

➤ Are you comfortable with the surgeon? Are they reputable? Have you seen examples of their work? A surgeon can be very good with facelifts but not so good with tummy tucks. Look at examples of the exact procedure you are planning to undertake.

➤ What about the clinic? To save on cost, some surgeons perform a number of these procedures in their office; I am sure that, in most cases, this is perfectly safe. I chose to have my surgery in hospital, surrounded by all the modern life-saving equipment and personnel. Where would you rather be if anything goes wrong?

➤ Are you comfortable with having surgery abroad? I did, but only because I am from Greece and the surgeon was highly recommended by women I knew well. Are you willing to go to a country where you don't know the customs or speak the language, have surgery, and then be sent home in a week? A lot of people do. I know of women who travel in pairs to support each other during recovery.

If you do decide to go abroad, you will need to do extra research on the hospital, the surgeon and the aftercare. Many hospitals have special departments that deal with medical tourism, which can assist you with any information or travel arrangements. I heard that one hospital in Trinidad has built special villas where you can stay during your recovery period.

➤ Finally, are you happy with the country's idea of beauty? There is a girl in my gym who came back from Colombia looking like an oversized

Barbie doll with a tiny waist over a grossly oversized bum. She loves it, but it may not be your cup of tea. South American doctors are well known for that look, yet you may want something more natural looking. The lower cost should not be your only consideration.

➢ How many procedures are you willing to have performed during the same surgery? You will be given options and you need to evaluate your tolerance for pain and inconvenience during recovery, as well as the risk of complications. Most women who go abroad tend to have at least two procedures at the same time. My surgeon discouraged me from doing so and in retrospect, I am very glad.

➢ How big or small or tight do you want to become? I took the advice of my surgeon and you should, too. They see thousands of bodies and have a pretty good idea of what will look good on you.

➢ How are your finances? Many places offer favourable credit options, especially in the UK. What is included in the proposal? Are there additional costs? Are you willing to pay more because of the posh location? Can you afford it?

There are many horror stories in the Daily Mail and similar publications about women who were butchered or even died during plastic surgery. Just recently, I read about a 39-year-old mother who went to Turkey, with the full support of her husband, for a "mummy makeover" (breast augmentation and tummy tuck). When she arrived, they offered her a freebie bum lift. This alone should have sent her running, in my view. The Brazilian butt lift is the deadliest of plastic surgery procedures, with 1 out of every 3000 women dying from embolism during surgery. Unfortunately for this woman, she agreed to the freebie; she ended up dying from a blood clot on the operating table when they injected fat from her tummy into her bum.

This and many other similar stories are terrifying and within the realm of surgery. To put the risks in perspective, the overall fatality rate for all hospital surgeries in the US is 1 out of every 500 patients. Deaths from anaesthesia (including elderly patients) is 1/13,000. Together, tummy tuck and liposuction procedures kill 1 in 5,000. Breast implants are the "safest", with 1/15,000 dying as a result of the procedure. By comparison, 1/10,000 dies during a normal vaginal delivery and 1/1,000 dies during a caesarean section.

Generally, I am in good health and I have had my share of surgeries, including two caesareans. Nevertheless, general anaesthesia and the mere thought of my skin getting willingly slashed, peeled away from the muscle and chopped up seemed a bit extreme, so I spent a lot of time pondering my options.

Neck Lift

I did have one area that bothered me so much that it ended up making the decision for me. The turkey neck! A common and pesky problem for many older women, the turkey neck is this bit of skin (or fat and skin) that goes from your chin straight to your chest, seemingly bypassing the natural curve of your throat. A well-defined jawline is a sign of youth and I wanted that.

To avoid the nuclear option, I explored the non-invasive – or should I say, less invasive – option of "threading". I will talk about threading in a later chapter; for now, all you need to know is that it was a complete and utter failure.

This left me with one last option, other than living the rest of my life in turtleneck jumpers. SURGERY! I was very fortunate to have been recommended a reputable plastic surgeon in my home town of Athens, Greece. I am not advocating here that you should have your surgery abroad, as many people have horrific experiences far away from home. However, in my case, it was a well- researched option in familiar surroundings, at a fraction of the cost of a similar procedure in the UK.

I had my daughter take several pictures of the hated profile and emailed them to the doctor, together with an extensive list of questions. I wanted to know about risks, pain level, recovery and the hospital stay, as well as the nitty gritty of the actual procedure. I am being truthful when I say that I did not overthink it.

Satisfied with the answers, I went ahead, sent a large deposit, and put an entry in my diary for a few months down the road. I knew that if I thought about it too much, I would postpone it from one month to the next and it would never happen. So, I jumped in head first...or should I say 'I stuck my neck out'?

The day arrived alarmingly quickly, and I found myself checking in to the clinic at 7am one March morning, three years ago. The staff were super-efficient, and I saw a string of doctors who checked my blood pressure, blood profile and heart rate, and took my medical history before showing me to my room. I changed into a hospital gown and by 8:30am, I was being wheeled in for surgery.

My surgeon took a few pictures (the befores) and a drop-dead gorgeous anaesthesiologist did her bit while a couple of nurses milled about the room. I was out like a light. In what seemed like a minute later, I was being woken by unfamiliar voices. It took a few seconds to remember where I was, and I was delighted that I felt no pain whatsoever.

Soon, I was in my room asking – actually, begging – for coffee. I was given none and told I had to wait three hours. This was the hardest part of the day! The hours passed, I was given a long-awaited coffee and after a couple of checks and instructions from the doctor, I was discharged to go home at 2pm. Admittedly, I looked a bit funny with a compression garment covering my whole head and neck like a tight hoodie. I wore a scarf over the whole thing and walked home.

The recovery was quick. I saw the doctor the next day and then went on vacation for a week. The most bothersome aspect was that I had to wear the compression garment 24/7 during that week, in order to help the skin adhere and heal nicely. On the fourth day, I took it off and had a wonderful shower, rinsing away all the dried blood from my hair. In fact, not knowing if I was allowed, I also applied a hair conditioning treatment that was divine.

I was clean for the first time in a week. I felt for the scars behind my ears and they seemed a little swollen, but nothing major. The girl that looked back at me from the mirror was 10 years younger. What I realised then, that I did not know previously, is that a neck lift also subtly lifts the bottom part of your face. The result was truly wonderful and I was over the moon.

Seven days later, the doctor did some final checks, removed the stitches and officially discharged me. Before flying off to England to parade the result, I also had Botox (to be discussed later). That was the end of the medical aspect.

I had minor nerve damage, a common side effect, which took a year to resolve completely. This made my smile slightly crooked in a way that annoyed me but seemed cheeky to others. For the first time in years, I was happy to be photographed in profile; in most pictures from that time and the next few months, you will see me in profile, while everyone else is smiling at the camera. I am simply delighted with the surgery results and would do it again in a heartbeat.

For the non-squeamish amongst you, the surgeon separated the skin from the muscle, pulled the muscle tight and then stuck the skin back on, snipping away all the excess. He then stitched the skin behind each ear, in an invisible scar.

To sum up: a neck lift will cost you between £2-£3K; the recovery is painless and quick; the result is very noticeable. I give this procedure a big thumbs up.

Breast Augmentation

Since I was a teenager, my breasts stubbornly refused to grow past an A-cup, also known as training bra-size. Being quite sporty, this did not bother me in the least. In fact, my breasts were one of the few body parts that I did not resent while growing up and in later life. Admittedly, after two pregnancies and breastfeeding two babies for a year each, I had been left with two sad-looking, drooping bags of skin, but I was still OK with it.

My wayward ex-husband used to say that he preferred small breasts, even though since he hightailed it, he has been spotted accompanying a substantial set of boobs attached to a blonde. The irony...

At any rate, a good push-up bra gave me a decent cleavage and in the dark, who cared? Turns out that somebody *did* care and my new boyfriend (clearly a boob man) complained bitterly about them. Affectionally, he whispered in my ear: "I stayed with you, despite your boobs." Having done the neck lift uneventfully and in the throes of excitement with my new romance, I decided to go ahead and fix the situation. I was also hoping for the operation to reduce the little bits of extra skin that seemed to be multiplying between my underarm and my bra (which were annoying me).

So, I made the appointment. Before long, I found myself being wheeled into surgery in a hospital gown. My surgeon, who is described as a magician when it comes to breasts, refused to discuss techniques, size or type of implant. Instead he wanted to know what result I was hoping for. He asked me if I was expecting to work as a porn star, which after a brief hesitation I dismissed as an option. Instead, I said that I work out a lot and I like to run. This is all he needed to know. He said he had a rough idea of the size, but he would make the final call on the operating table. For those of you who want to pick the size of the implant, I strongly advise you to let your surgeon decide. He has done it many times and knows what will suit your frame best. Just give him an idea of the look you want to achieve.

I remember waking up from surgery and looking down at my proudly-standing twin globes and thinking "Wow!" Then they concealed the little miracles under bandages and I did not see them again for a few days. I spent one night in hospital and I had no pain, but I did throw up a couple of times, probably reacting to the anaesthesia.

At home, I was OK to do most things, including getting up and out of bed without pain. I am quite fit, and I believe this helped. If you are not very fit, a few pillows under your back will help you roll out of bed just as easily. A day later, I had my check-up and the doctor removed the bandages. He helped me put on a D-size sports bra which I had to keep on 24/7 for about a month. There were two very small incisions under the breasts, and they were completely hidden. As it transpires, breasts go down in size during that month, so my final size once all was said and done ended up being a C. I am quite short and petite so a C was ample, but not excessive. He had picked the perfect size.

My view overall is that it was an easy procedure, with minimal pain and good recovery, highly recommended if you have deflated, pitifully saggy boobs. I am often asked if my breasts feel hard or unnatural, which they did for the first few months. Now they feel completely natural and part of me. The NHS is fully accommodating, scheduling my mammograms with nurses who are trained to handle implants.

I never thought that having a breast augmentation would be a big deal, but I have changed my mind since. Men and women (mostly women) stare longingly at my cleavage when I walk by, my waist looks smaller and I can wear anything without a bra. They never go unnoticed and my eyes have been opened to the power of the boob. Now, I love them – small enough to exercise and run without jiggling and big enough to give me an amazing bikini body. The extra skin between my armpits and bra has disappeared and I am a true convert. Did I already mention how much I love them? Ladies, if you have breasts like mine, you will not regret this procedure.

A funny thing that happened in surgery...

As I was being wheeled out of surgery in my dazed post-anaesthesia state, I noticed a lot of pitiful glances directed my way. I did not know what to make of this, until I had a look in the mirror later on. My face was bright red, like a burn victim. Turns out that while I was under anaesthesia, my surgeon decided to give me an early Christmas present in the form of a free needling treatment. The nurses and patients thought that I was in surgery to treat my severely burned face. That aside, I was of course very grateful, and you will see why in later chapters.

To sum up: a breast augmentation will cost between £3-£4K, the pain is minimal, and the recovery is quite easy. The look and feel are amazing. Big thumbs up.

Tummy Tuck with Liposuction

I decided to have a tummy tuck primarily because I was emboldened by the success of the neck lift and the boob job. The great result, together with the quick recovery and minimal pain, made me decide to work on my bikini body.

I did not make the decision lightly. A tummy tuck is one of the most extensive and complicated plastic surgery procedures, with the most pain and the longest recovery. A little word of caution here: I asked my doctor to do it together with the boob job in what is affectionally labelled the "mummy makeover", but he advised strongly against the combined operation. His professional opinion is that the recovery, pain and risk of infection is too great. It's very popular in America, but you may want to give it a miss.

Similarly to the other two procedures, I checked into the hospital at 7am and went through all the medical checks. When pronounced healthy enough, I was wheeled into surgery. The surgeon said that he would fine-tune the result with a bit of liposuction and I was grateful. He marked my belly with a black marker while I was standing up, and then they knocked me out. The operation lasted four hours and it involved cutting out my old caesarean scars, as well as relocating my belly button. This had to be done, as he cut out a piece of skin in the shape of a smile across from the belly button and from hip to hip.

When I woke up, I felt relieved and I was not in pain. I was given plenty of codeine, and it worked very well. I had two drains coming out of my pubic area, draining the fluid that accumulated between the muscles and the skin. Pretty gross, eh?

That first night was the hardest. I had to sleep sitting up, so as not to put pressure on the incision. I will not lie to you, I was up for a good part of the night. Curiously, the most intense agony was a leg cramp that kept shooting arrows of red-hot pain up my thigh. I was not allowed out of bed that first night and this made the cramp much worse. The disgusting bags at the end of the drains added to the discomfort and the terrible food made me want to cry. Despite all that, I was happy it was over and did not regret any of it.

The next morning, I was allowed up, but I had to walk like the hunchback of Notre Dame to avoid damaging the incision. The leg pain was still there, but the walking helped. Practicalities, primarily surrounding the drains and baggies, were further difficulties to contend with.

Prior to the operation, I had bought a lot of supplies to help with healing and recovery, such as scar gels, silicone sheets, Bio-Oil, etc. I had also ordered a special scar prevention system called "Embrace" which had to come from America and a selection of corsets and loose nighties. Turns out I did not need any of that for several weeks as I was put in a bulletproof hospital corset, which I was to wear 24/7 for the next month. This contraption helped establish the new shape of my waist and tummy and kept the swelling down, but I will not lie to you, it was uncomfortable. In fact, it was probably what I hated the most about this procedure.

When I took it off, my body complained bitterly, so there was no way out...*literally*. Once the month had passed, I was gradually able to wear my more comfortable corsets. I slowly hit the gym as well, but for several months afterwards I needed to resort to the hospital corset to control the swelling from time to time.

Swelling is one of the main complications of a tummy tuck. Fluid accumulates, which is meant to go through the drains. In my case, the drains were removed after three days. This was quick and painless and was done at the doctor's office.

After two days in the hospital, I was allowed home for a week's rest. I had stocked the flat with goodies, books I had meant to read for ages, and was kind of looking forward to this enforced rest. Unfortunately, it was not as enjoyable as I had envisioned. The corset was a constant nuisance and the leg cramps were ever present. What truly helped was joining a tummy tuck support Facebook group. It is extremely active, especially with Americans, and it gives you a good idea of the variety of healing times and complications. If you decide to join such a group, I suggest you do so *after* your procedure. Some of the stories there will make your hair stand on end, but they are the exception and some of them are a bit dramatized.

The week passed, and I was able to walk upright, the disgusting baggies and drains were gone (but had left two little round scars behind, which are still there), and the doctor was happy to discharge me to go home with instructions on how to care for the incision. Before our final goodbyes, he did remove the stitches and about half a pint of fluid using a ginormous syringe which he plunged into my belly. As gruesome as this looked it did not hurt a bit, as the whole area was numb.

Back home, I continued to worry about the fluid and emailed him several times, but he said it would be absorbed by the body, which it eventually was. As soon as the scar dried up and stopped weeping, I started using the Bio-Oil and the silicone sheets. Once a month had passed, I started using the incredibly pricey Embrace bandage ($500 for 60 days' supply) imported from America. It is meant to make your scars almost disappear. I wore it for ten days at a time, with a day's rest in-between and followed all instructions religiously, but I am not so sure that it made enough of a difference to warrant the cost. The scar gel was useless but massaging the Bio-Oil helped, I think. I also did a ten-course of lymphatic massage which kept the swelling down.

A month later, I started going to the gym, using a tight neoprene belt around my waist and covering the incision. It took about a week before I could do many of the exercises, and a month before I could go back to doing abdominal crunches and Pilates. I wore the belt at the gym for the next eight months and still do, occasionally. I also wore a regular corset under my clothes for four months. The key with a tummy tuck recovery is compression to reduce swelling and strain on the scar as well as to force your body into its new post-liposuction shape.

A year later, I paraded my truly spectacular tummy in a bikini at St. Tropez and all the discomfort was forgotten. I have a hip to hip scar that still looks a bit brownish but is completely hidden below the bikini line. My belly button has a little scar covered nicely by my new belly button piercing. I suppose a tummy tuck operation is unlike anything else you will read about in this book in terms of recovery. Would I do it again? Unequivocally, the answer is yes.

A quick note on belly button piercing...

It's not for everyone and I got mine during a moment of madness at a Camden tattoo parlour. Just before the summer, and as I was approaching the end of my arduous tummy tuck recovery, I decided to do it on the spur of the moment. All my gym buddies seemed to have one (OK, I live in chav territory) and after months of endless ab exercises, I felt that I deserved one. Having it done was painful and also hurt sporadically for the next few months. In fact, almost a year later, I still get the odd stabbing pain when it gets caught on tights or high-waisted pants. During the first few months, I lived in constant fear of infection, as you are not meant to go swimming for a month and I totally ignored that rule. On the whole, I love how it looks, and having it done put my two teenage daughters off piercings for life, but I would not do it again. The hassle is too much.

To sum up: a tummy tuck is a major operation with significant recovery time. The cost varies greatly from £4-£9K and the results are spectacular. Together with a bit of exercise, you will have a better looking belly than most twenty-year-olds and wearing a bikini will be a viable option again.

STRENGTH TRAINING

Many of the suggestions in this book are pricey and involve doctors and beauty therapists. Strength training is already included in any gym membership and is a must-have, not only for getting toned arms and perky behinds but also for your overall health.

There are volumes of research proving that resistance or strength training is the best way to retain your body mass and strong bones. You can do this with the machines at the gym, with free weights or by taking a Bodypump or HIIT class.

Muscles need calories, so a toned body tends to stay thinner. Win-win! If you are not a person who goes to the gym willingly, I recommend that you hire a personal trainer to get you started or find a gym buddy, so you can motivate each other.

I could wax lyrical about exercise, as I think it is a life-or-death decision (that's how serious I am about exercise), but I won't because the subject has been covered extensively and exhaustively in numerous publications. Instead, I will offer you below a little nugget that I discovered on my own.

Body Combat and Bingo Wings

There are three solutions to bingo wings: hide them and never reveal your full arms again; plastic surgery with quite ugly scars running down your arms; and a once-a-week body combat class. If you do not know what this is, don't fret, it does not involve actual body combat. You punch and kick the air for about 50 minutes, choreographed to music. There is something about this particular form of exercise that targets bingo wings and it is the only one that I have found to work in that particular area.

LASER EYE SURGERY

My eyes gave up the ghost gradually, starting from the age of 45 or so. Distance did not become a problem, but reading a book or a small smartphone screen was beginning to prove challenging. Reading glasses perched on the tip of one's nose scream "grandma!" and do not create a good look in the best of circumstances. More importantly, being an avid reader, I found that the pile of books by the side of my bed became higher and higher, primarily because reading was a struggle.

When my arm became too short to hold a book at reading distance and my restaurant choices were narrowed to "just order me what you think I'd like", I knew that I had to do something about it. I needed the sort of solution that would not only fix the distance problem (which can be easily corrected by any laser surgery), but also the near-reading issue.

After lots of research I found an eye clinic in London that pioneered a solution called LASIK Blended Vision for patients who are 45+. The actual procedure took less than ten minutes and was completely painless. I walked out of their office, several thousand pounds lighter, but with better vision than I have had in years. I have not needed any type of glasses since that day and I can read any menu or book without strain. It is a miracle!

I would like to reassure any of you who are nervous at the thought of a beam of laser pointed at your eye. I was too. In fact, I did not have laser surgery in my twenties when everyone around me was having it, despite being very, very near-sighted. I was simply terrified at the thought. Glasses and contacts were good enough for me, thank you very much...but now they weren't doing their job any more.

Here is my experience of this procedure. To begin with, they did loads of measurements and tests and I was told to not use contacts for one week. On the day, the nurse put a dashing hairnet on my head and took my glasses away. I walked into a room with a seat that looked like a dentist's chair. Above the door was a sign that I could not read. The eye surgeon fitted me with a contraption that kept my eyes open. This is what I was afraid of the most. Then he said that I could blink if I wanted. Sure enough, even though there was no way I could actually blink, it felt like I could, and this made all the difference in the world.

One of my eyes was weaker than the other and took a minute longer to zap. I saw disco lights, but it did not hurt. I could smell something burning but did not really want to ask what it was, or even speculate on the origin. Ten minutes later, I got up and walked out, throwing my glasses in a large fishbowl next to the surgery. The nurse pointed at the sign over the doorway that I could not read earlier.

It said: "Ten minutes ago I could not read this."

HIFU (HIGH FREQUENCY ULTRASOUND)

Oh, the pain! This is not a procedure for the faint-hearted. In fact, many doctors refuse to buy the machine, because despite the efficiency of the treatment, the pain is so intense that patients flee halfway through the session and many never complete the course. Local anaesthetic does not reach the deeper layers where HIFU does its work, so the only slight relief comes with paracetamol or codeine. Anti-inflammatory drugs are not recommended as the inflammation of these deeper layers is what causes the collagen production, the ultimate purpose of the treatment.

I was introduced to the idea as I was lying face-down on a massage bed in a pair of very skimpy paper panties, getting my behind lifted with a treatment that I will discuss later on. I was idly looking around, asking the therapist about the different machines in my line of vision. The HIFU machine looked innocent enough and the whole idea behind it is at the heart of what most rejuvenation treatments try to do these days. The fight seems to have moved on from treating the top layers of the skin with creams and facials to targeting the deeper layers with lasers, ultrasound, needling and ingestible collagen. The HIFU machine, as the name suggests, uses high frequency ultrasound to injure the deeper layers of the skin and force them to produce more collagen, which in turn plumps up the skin and banishes the wrinkles.

When I got home, I went on *realself.com* (which is the oracle on every cosmetic treatment, by the way) and read about HIFU. Everyone seemed to mention the pain, but the promised results appeared little short of miraculous. The cost of three recommended treatments ran a little over £1K, so nothing to sneeze at. In the spirit of my quest to try everything that has proven its efficiency, I soon found myself at the therapist's bench, quivering in fear with my eyes shut tight. I had taken a modest dose of paracetamol half an hour before the start of the procedure.

In the first session, she targeted the eye area. It started innocently enough, with an absolutely lovely face massage and deep cleanse. But I was not fooled, I knew there was more to come. Once my face was thoroughly cleaned and scrubbed, she picked up a probe and started with the treatment. The sensation is hard to forget. The best way to describe the feeling is that of a hammer hitting the inside of your skull. It only lasted 20 minutes but every second hurt intensely, and as she went over the same area it got worse. Like hitting your head at the corner of a table and then going back for more. During the treatment, I knew that nothing, absolutely *nothing* would convince me to go back for the other two treatments. I understood completely why others before me had bolted, never to return.

The therapist was really brilliant, reminding me of my midwife during childbirth. "Come on Sasha," she cajoled, "you are doing great!" Her soothing manner was what carried me through the rest of the procedure, as well as the knowledge that even one treatment is quite effective. Sure enough, I was not coming back for more.

A month passed, the recommended time between treatments, and my resolve started to weaken as I saw startling results. All the little wrinkles around the eye area first softened, then disappeared. The next treatment was meant to target the mouth area and I had already paid for it. Would I forfeit the money? Should I not suck it up and go? I managed to extract a codeine prescription out of my GP and decided to man up.

The same treatment around the mouth area hurt significantly less. The sensation resembled that of having your teeth cleaned with ultrasounds by an army-trained dental hygienist. The codeine seemed to dull the worst of it and I felt brave enough to schedule the last treatment.

A month later, having swallowed my codeine pill, I waited for the dull sensation of the hammers to hit my forehead. Alas, despite the codeine, the pain was just as bad as the first time; I discovered quite late in the day that my milder previous experience had to do with the treatment area, rather than the pain relief.

In conclusion: the HIFU is a truly diabolical machine with miraculous results. I will leave this one up to you.

WARDROBE OVERHAUL

Clothes are tricky, and how you dress gives away your age. My wardrobe used to be full of black suits (my work uniform in the City) and a variety of outdated and unflattering casual clothes. It was chock full of scarves, bolts, shoes and other accessories that had not seen the light of day since the 19th century. In the depths of it, I even discovered a complete pink bunny outfit that I had picked up in a car boot sale (God knows why).

When I embarked on a clear-out, more than half of what I had was easily discarded with no outside advice. I was ruthless, and it took all day in front of a full-length mirror. Anything that didn't fit right, gone! I also threw out any clothes that I had kept over the years, hoping that someday I would be that size again. As a friend of mine pointed out: "If you lose weight, surely you will want to go shopping. Why keep these old things?"

Another category that was hard to part with – but I discarded anyway – included my lounging around, bag lady clothes. We all have them. Comfortable, stretched out and faded sweatpants and jumpers, whose only merit is that we can curl up on the sofa and eat unlimited amounts of junk without feeling a shred of discomfort. As it happens, these clothes have a sinister way of making it out of the house…initially for a quick trip to the supermarket or the post office and eventually, as we age, further afield. GONE!

I did not forget the underwear and sock drawer, where carnage ensued; any greying and fraying items went in the bin, regardless of how comfortable they were. Belts and shoes that did not fit right or had gone out of fashion when I was in my twenties were also discarded.

With my wardrobe severely pruned, next came the difficult part where I had to get outside help. I chose my best-dressed girlfriends in the 30-40 age group and with a bottle of prosecco – and a lot of patience – we went through the rest of my wardrobe and created outfits that worked. Surprisingly, there was some life left in the old wardrobe, but many items still did not make the cut.

As I got older, the colours that worked in my younger days now made me look pale and drawn. Mostly everything black had to go and only a few dark blues survived. This may be different for you depending on your colouring, but matte black is generally a "no" for all women over 40. Joining the "no" pile was anything that could be described as girly and cute, bows on anything, any clothes involving a bib, leopard print, very high heels…and unfortunately, the little black dress. I did a final pass of the remaining clothes in front of my disinterested partner. With some prodding, he admitted to the clothes he did not like to see me in, and those items joined the charity bag.

A quick word about black

Black does not do any favours for older women. This comes from someone who used to love black, and everything in my closet was black or midnight blue. It took a lot of convincing to ditch the black and I still look longingly at the racks of little black dresses, but I finally had to admit that it made me look drawn and old beyond my years. I now wear colours that I would not have touched in the past and the look is really good. I have been experimenting with red, mustard, forest green and light grey. If you are a junkie for black like I was, moderate it and you will be surprised by how many compliments you get.

Shopping

Then came the fun part: shopping! But don't do it alone. Take the voice of reason along – in my case, a willing victim who volunteered for the task. Up and down Oxford street we went for a full day. I came away from the shopping trip with a few items that I loved, and my friend also agreed. Thanks to advancements in technology, I was able to double-check our choices with my partner at home.

We did most of the shopping at Zara, which has a great selection of stylish clothes for the 30-40 group. Even though my advice is to stay away from shops that cater to my daughters, I did pick up a couple of tops from Forever 21. We determined that the colours that suit me are most greens, some reds, light grey, most shades of brown, butterscotch (go figure) and plum; not a one of these colours would I have worn in the past, yet they make such a difference to how I look and feel.

We also looked at my shape. I have wide shoulders, a short waist and long legs. Jacket shopping was challenging, but most low-waisted clothes looked great. Let your body decide the fashion, rather than try to squeeze yourself into trendy items that do not suit you.

Once you get to be a certain age, fashion faux pas can make you look older. Some of your more unfortunate choices can also make you look ridiculous. Enlist the help of others until you are well practiced, as we tend to see a much younger person in the mirror with our mind's eye.

To sum up: your wardrobe can age you by decades if it is not evaluated, updated and pruned regularly. On the plus side, a well-chosen wardrobe can take decades off your age and flatter you well below your years.

MASSIVE CHANGE WITH LOW EFFORT AND POSSIBLY LOW COST

HAIR DYE

Many praise a full head of shiny grey or white hair and marvel at the self-confidence and liberation of the lady that dares to go grey. To me, greys scream "grandmother", and as much as I adored my *nona* (who by the way religiously highlighted hers well into her nineties), I personally will never be seen with grey roots – or any roots, for that matter. Nothing gives the game away faster than grey hair.

Of course, this is quite curious as many people get their first greys in their early thirties; nevertheless, and perhaps due to popular culture, grey hair normally sits atop a wrinkled lady sitting by the fire.

If you want to quickly knock fifty years off your age, do your roots on a regular basis, normally every four to five weeks. I have discovered two ways to extend this to eight weeks and both are available at your local pharmacy.

One is a wonderful product that comes with hair dye and a little brush. The innovation is that there are only a few shades with one guaranteed to match yours and once applied on the roots, it only takes 10 minutes to do its magic. It fades quicker than regular hair colour, but you only need to get a couple of weeks out of it.

The other product, I normally use in an emergency. This can happen as grey hairs, unlike regular hairs, can appear overnight and without warning. A quick spritz on the roots and they are gone until the next shampoo.

A quick word about hair colour

As we age, it is important to re-evaluate our hair colour. What looked good in your twenties can make you look drawn and tired in your fifties. Normally, a softer variant of what suits your skin colour and features will frame your face better and knock off a few years. A few highlights give bounce to flat, lifeless hair. Too many and it becomes difficult and expensive to do your roots every few weeks. I often see a beautiful set of highlights completely ruined by a few inches of grey roots. So, keep an eye on maintenance when you make your decision.

Blue, pink, purple and any variant of these colours should never be an option past your late teens. I am not sure what is happening with the world, but lately, I have seen middle-aged women sporting these colours and the look is always one of a crazy cat lady.

For most people, a colour close to their natural one is the best choice.

HAIR EXTENSIONS

Countless books have been written about hair and the difference it can make to the overall appearance of a woman. Good hair is instantly noticeable and can draw attention away from other, less desirable features. For that reason, you need to think carefully about what you do with your locks.

Men and women alike love long, luscious hair, yet many women get some sort of pixie cut as soon as they hit their forties. This sort of boyish cut is very ageing and should be avoided. I never got one of those cuts willingly and always dreamed of swishing my long, glorious hair in the breeze.

Unfortunately, the most I ever got was shoulder-length hair that tapered off into a pitiful rat tail. Because of this inability of my hair to reach the desired length in a decent state, I always kept it just below my shoulders and full of assorted products that briefly made it look full (for about 2 hours). After a short-lived and out of character revival during my two pregnancies, my hair started thinning and looking a bit drab and lifeless. Age has a way of cutting in many different ways.

A daily dose of collagen and a revolutionary hair treatment called Olaplex (both discussed further down) have given new life to my locks. So much so that I decided to go with the flow and try out hair extensions, partly for added length but primarily for extra volume.

A word of caution here: too long is as bad as too short when it comes to hair and ageing. Stay within reason and avoid going longer than waist length, at all costs. I chose 16" length with highlights to match my own.

The broad consensus amongst those who know me is that hair extensions are the best anti-ageing strategy I have tried. Guys in particular absolutely love my waist-length tresses, and so do I! Easy to style, no need for regular haircuts or frequent shampooing, what is there to argue about?

There are many methods to attach extensions and I chose the weave with two tracks. This looks the best and it is invisible, even with "updos" and on windy days. There are many other ways to attach extensions and choosing the wrong one can do a lot of damage to your natural hair. Do your research, like I did mine, as they all have their pros and cons. I have found a fantastic salon that specialises in black hair. They are super-experienced when it comes to weaves, and they know what to look for and where to best place the tracks. The cost is also a fraction of the posh salon I went to originally.

Buying the actual hair is the biggest expense. Hand-made extensions with real hair are the best. Each hair is attached facing the same direction and the track is thinner and lighter. Expect to pay several hundred pounds for the actual extensions and they will last two to three years, if you condition them properly. I condition mine once a week. Other than that, I use a sun protection spray in the summer and tie them in a loose plait at night.

What I have found hardest about having hair extensions is sleeping. The first two nights are always the most difficult and it feels like you are sleeping on large pebbles. After that, it feels like you are sleeping on small pebbles. When it feels like you are sleeping on a pillow, you know it is time to go back to the hairdresser and reattach them. On occasion, you may also get a maddening itch deep in your skull and if you do not dry them properly at the roots, you will soon have a slight musty smell emanating from your luscious locks.

Despite these drawbacks, when I first got my extensions, I was so happy – and the compliments so sincere – that I kept them on for six months straight. Just to clarify, the hairdresser would take them off every four weeks and reattach them closer to the roots, at a slightly different location to avoid stressing the same area. This, together with a hair conditioning treatment, would take less than two hours (10 minutes to remove, 30 minutes for the treatment, 40 minutes to reattach the tracks, and 20 minutes to style). I was so addicted to the look that I travelled far and wide to find a hairdresser during my summer vacation in a very remote area of Greece.

What put a stop to wearing them continuously was the discovery of a bald spot the size of a pea. Apparently, your hair needs a few weeks' break between applications to recover, which is what I do now. I used a special shampoo to help it grow faster and I have bought a great set of clip-on extensions for when I go out. My long-term strategy is to grow my own hair to the desired length, and then just use a few hair extensions for volume to minimise discomfort while maintaining the look.

BOTOX

Botox is the staple of anti-ageing. A few quick jabs and ten years leave your face (only to return 3-6 months later). It has become so popular that my dentist is offering it at the same time as teeth cleaning. I am hearing more and more from people in their twenties that they are having Botox to prevent wrinkles from ever appearing, which by the way is a crazy way to spend your money. Botox has a toxin that temporarily paralyses the muscles in your forehead and around your eyes. This makes your face relax and keeps you from frowning, and looking sad or angry.

As we get older, life's worries sculpt a permanent frown on our foreheads. A worry-lined face is not a good look. As the saying goes: "Frown, and the world frowns with you." Botox to the rescue…and it even appears to do so much more!

A recent article in Psychology Today discussed a study where seriously depressed patients were given Botox. Two months later, nine out of ten no longer appeared depressed in standard depression tests evaluated by doctors. They also discovered in a separate study that people who had received Botox had a blunted reaction to feelings of anger and sadness, but it did not affect their reaction to happy feelings.

Now, I don't want to get your hopes up that you will ditch the Prozac and start skipping around like a newborn lamb in spring, but there is some evidence that this can happen once you physically cannot get angry. Having been an angry person myself, I am finding that I am much more relaxed and smiley these days.

In terms of the actual treatment, it is pretty much painless. The doctor uses local anaesthetic, and injects all the small (and large) wrinkles on your forehead and around your eyes with a very fine needle. Botox can only work on the top half of your face; fillers, which are discussed in the next section, take care of the lower half.

The whole needle-jabbing part takes less than five minutes and it takes 24-48 hours before you see the result. There is no down time, but you are not allowed to lie down for a few hours after the procedure. Again, I suggest that you go to a professional to achieve a natural, yet unlined result.

In my case, Botox lasts about four months, which is average, and the cost can vary depending on how many areas you want treated (approx. £100/area). My advice is to leave it up to the doctor to decide what will look good on you.

FILLERS

If you want to look five years younger in five minutes with very little pain, fillers are the way to go. Marionette lines and the deep creases from under your nose to the top of your mouth will magically disappear. If your doctor is as good as mine, he will make all the tiny lines on the upper lip disappear too. In that area, my doctor used *Teosyal RHA1*.

Fillers in the upper cheek areas are also quite magical. Pictures before and after literally look like pictures taken ten years apart. This has been called the liquid facelift and I can attest that fillers in the cheek area fully deserve the name. I had *Teosyal Ultra Deep* but there are other brands that can be equally effective, such as *Juvéderm Voluma*.

I cannot stress enough the importance of having this done by a doctor and not a nurse or beautician. I have seen women turn into trouts after going to unqualified practitioners. This is an unregulated market in the UK, so do your homework.

In terms of the actual procedure, the doctor applies numbing cream thirty minutes beforehand. Once it takes effect, he uses a tiny needle to expertly fill all the deeper wrinkles (as well as the tiny creases) with hyaluronic acid, banishing all imperfections. Hyaluronic acid is a natural agent found in the skin and because it absorbs moisture, it gives the skin a plump and hydrated look. The procedure is painless, and the results are instant. There is no swelling, but you may get a little bruising if you bruise easily.

Fillers can be used in other areas, such as the hands and the lips. I cannot attest to the effectiveness of any of those as I have not tried them (yet). Fillers last from 12-18 months before they are absorbed by the body, but I tend to go every 6 months to banish all the new wrinkles that make their appearance. Magic!

PERMANENT MAKEUP

As we age, the natural outline of our lips sort of blends in with the rest of the face and loses the well-defined shape of our younger days. Thinning eyebrows are another sign of ageing. They can get unruly and may even become grey. If you grew up in the 80s, like I did, you probably waxed and tweezed them into a thin line that refuses to regain its previous bushy glory.

Permanent makeup to the rescue. To be perfectly honest, ageing was not what originally drew me to this procedure, even though it ended up having a significant uplifting effect when all was said and done. When it comes to makeup, I am lazy.

Well into my thirties, the only items I possessed were an eyeliner pencil and a few lipsticks (and many expired samples that came with Christmas gifts). The thought of never having to put on makeup or wake up bare-faced was very appealing. I had recently taken to making my brows darker and thicker, and I found that the look was excellent when I bothered to do it. So, my first thought was about tattooing my eyebrows. When I researched the topic, I discovered that the correct term for what I wanted done is "microblading".

And here is the warning: *what you are doing is letting someone semi-permanently tattoo your face.* Groupon and cut-price outfits are not the places to seek this sort of procedure. If you decide to go ahead, you must do your research and pay top price for the best there is. I found my therapist through recommendation. She has a very extensive social media presence, so I had a chance to look through hundreds of pictures of her work before agreeing to go ahead. Her walls were covered with certificates and even though she looked about twelve years old, the certificates were dated several years back. She had a wonderful manner about her, and her schedule was chock full for several weeks in advance. All these are good signs when you are about to allow ink-covered needles near your eyeballs.

Microblading gave me an instant brow lift, it defined my features and framed my face by opening up my eyes. Now for the not so great parts...

It hurt! And it took forever! I was there getting intricately pierced with vibrating needles and razor blades for a total of five hours, and this was only for the brows and lips. I read that the first pass hurts the most because the anaesthetic cannot penetrate the skin and do its magic. This is true, but the rest of the procedure is no picnic either. Some areas don't hurt at all and others are really sensitive, so if you are going to do it, go with your eyes open. You will have to close them when you are there and try to think of your favourite things...

When it is all finished, do not look in the mirror, as everything will appear so dark that you will look like the devil's bride. My lips were swollen to twice their size and my eyebrows were two solid black slashes. Not a good look. The therapist was not at all ruffled by my reaction and sent me home with a stash of instructions and sachets of balm.

It took a week before I could see what the final result would look like, and I was absolutely delighted. Once the scabs fell off, everything softened, and the most beautiful lips emerged under eyebrows that could only have been drawn by Michelangelo. I was over the moon.

It was this enthusiasm that gave me the courage to not only go back for my free touch-up six weeks later, but to also submit to the most feared of permanent makeup procedures (at least for me): the permanent eyeliner. I will not bore you with the details, but the "touch-up" was a full two hours, very much reminiscent of the original torture. As for the eyelids… This truly hurt, and I bled and bled. In total, I was there for six long hours. And it was totally worth it. The beautifully drawn cat's eyes uplift my whole face and look amazing.

The only real downside is that permanent makeup is not really permanent. You will need to go back every year or two for what is euphemistically called a touch-up, but is really a full-blown torture session. On the plus side, you will be waking up and walking around with Hollywood-standard makeup that most women could not hope to duplicate on their own efforts.

NEEDLING

If you have never heard of this, it is a pen-looking device; at one end, as the name suggests, it has several sharp needles that retract and extend at a predetermined depth. The doctor runs this all over your face (and other areas, where needed) and turns you into a bloody mess. The needles puncture the top layers of the skin and drive vitamin A cream into the deeper layers. Your body gets really upset about the carnage and produces loads of collagen to repair the damage. The result, after a few days, is fresher, younger-looking skin that glows.

My doctor claims that of all the therapies that are available for rejuvenation, this is the only one he uses on himself and his wife. He looks quite good and every time I see him, I always ask if he's had Botox...

A series of four sessions once a year will achieve and maintain the desired result. They need to be done in the winter, as you must stay out of the sun for two weeks after the procedure and even then, the recommendation is that you cover yourself in some serious sun cream. You will have pronounced redness for 24 hours, gradually tapering off after five days. This redness is easily covered with foundation.

Micro-needling also worked very well on my tummy tuck scar, and even made a difference with a decade-old scar on my arm. A few days after the procedure, there was slight peeling and the skin underneath revealed itself to be clearly plumper and brighter. The doctor says that our bodies evolved to be able to repair scratches and wounds sustained as our ancestors ran through the jungle and scraped themselves. For this reason, he recommends that I avoid chemical peels and stick to mechanical damage. It makes sense to me.

Of course, there is a cumulative effect from everything I have done, but some treatments work positively better than others. Needling is definitely one of the better ones and I have added it to my regular routine.

EYELASH EXTENSIONS

Wake up beautiful! Warning, warning, warning!!!! Eyelash extensions are highly addictive and expensive (at least for the good ones).

As we age, our eyelashes become sparse and the eyes get a hooded appearance, which makes them look smaller (and you, older). Eyelash extensions have a dramatic impact on your face. They open up your eyes and make them look brighter and more awake.

For those of you who do not know what this is, it is a process during which a technician glues individual eyelashes onto your natural eyelashes, one by one. I have mine done at home, snoozing on my bed. The whole thing takes about one hour, and the results are quite amazing.

Depending on how much you are willing to pay, you can get eyelashes made of mink or synthetic ones. I started with the cheap ones and worked my way to the mink ones, as I found out that the cheap ones are a false economy as they don't last as long, make my eyes itch and are a bit heavier. If you don't rub your eyes, they can last several weeks. Mine last about five weeks, and I have been wearing them continuously for three and a half years. As the weeks go by, your natural lashes shed, and the expensive mink ones shed with them.

An additional bonus is that you quickly learn to avoid rubbing or otherwise torturing the eye area. This is a very good habit to have, as the skin around the eyes is very thin and messing with it makes it sag and complain in myriad different ways.

At this stage, I would also like to dispel a myth. You may have heard that eyelash extensions damage your own lashes. There is absolutely no proof that they do. What happens is that after you get used to seeing yourself with your amazing lashes, once they are off you look a bit like a balding chicken. Your natural lashes are all still there, you just forgot how pitiful they are. What happens is that they shed naturally, and with them go the expensive mink ones.

Now for the look! Eyelash extensions have been called the new facelift for women over fifty. Not only do they look completely natural, but a set of full, flirty eyelashes will make you look younger by giving your face a lifted look. If you are like me and do not care to spend hours on your makeup, these lashes will give you an amazing look with minimal effort.

8 MINUTE ABS

OK ladies, who is up for some great abs? I discovered the 8 Minute Abs YouTube video through my boyfriend. One fine morning early on in the relationship, when all was hot and heavy, he jumped out of bed, fired up YouTube and invited me to join him in what can only be described as eight painful minutes, also known as 8 Minute Abs. I was surprised, but I persevered and soon saw the benefits.

The key to success, like with any exercise, lies with incorporating it into your daily routine. It is ONLY eight minutes, you can slot it in anytime during the day. I do my 8 Minute Abs in the morning, barefoot and in my pyjamas. There are several levels, but I have been stuck on Level 2 for three years. Never mind, it does the job. How do I know? Firstly, the abs are looking good...you may pipe up to say that this is because of the tummy tuck, which is true as far as the extra skin is concerned. But when my surgeon opened up my tummy and took a peek inside, he was amazed by the set of abs that he uncovered.

Call me vain, but I do like to wear bikinis and I also love the tight belt feeling around my waist. On a practical note, a strong core is useful in so many ways, including getting out of bed easily after surgery, sport, and several daily tasks that are made difficult as you get older.

There is absolutely no excuse to not dedicate eight minutes a day to this very important muscle group – which, by the way, can be exercised every day, unlike the rest of your muscles. As an extra bonus, your awesome abs will attract attention away from any parts of your body which are not so awesome and cannot be exercised as effectively.

Convinced?

SKINADE

This works! And it is only your wallet that will hurt from the daily drinkable dose of collagen. There are a few other small drawbacks that require some scheduling on your part. Skinade needs to be consumed at least one hour before or an hour after coffee. Also, it works best on an empty stomach. I tried several combinations, including having some herbal tea in the morning while counting the minutes for the hour to pass, but it was pure torture. I have now settled into having the premixed Skinade near my bed, and I suck it down when I wake up to stumble to the bathroom for my early morning bathroom visit. I have been taking it for a year and the habit is set.

There has been a lot of talk around ingestible beauty and several companies have come up with their version of collagen supplements. The price reflects the ingredients and Skinade is undisputedly the reigning queen of the lot, and the only one with significant clinical research to prove its effectiveness. There are also over 2000 verified reviews on Trustpilot that have given it a rating of 4.8/5.

I started with a course of 90 days and saw a significant difference in my skin, hair and nails after taking it religiously for a month. By 90 days, I could see a difference in my hands. There is no beating about the bush here, it simply works! My skin feels plumper, is dewy and looks radiant. I have new little hairs growing on my head like when I was pregnant and people that have not seen me in a while are commenting positively. I will not do without my daily Skinade, about the cost of a daily Starbucks coffee. It goes with me everywhere and I absolutely love the results.

HRT (HORMONE REPLACEMENT THERAPY)

Menopause was relatively kind to me, and I soldiered on without any medical assistance. I had hot flushes, but they were not terrible. My hair went a bit lank, my body shape changed to a waistless banana and my wicked temper flared on a regular basis for no reason...but other than those minor inconveniences, I was coping OK.

Then started the sleeping torture. I would fall asleep easily but it never quite felt like I was fully asleep. Instead, I lingered on the edge of consciousness most of the night, and would wake up often before falling back asleep. Now, I don't know about you, but I have always been a fabulous sleeper, so much so that not even the desperate cries of my baby daughters pierced through my blissful slumber. This sleeping problem was what sent me to the doctor in search of a solution.

Slightly embarrassed and feeling like a wimp, I meekly asked the doctor about HRT. "I don't really need it, I am doing fine, but this sleeping disturbance is a bit annoying. What do you think?" Without looking up, she said crisply: "Let's get you onto HRT then, shall we?"

And with those words, my life changed...

After a few more questions and going through some stats, I went home clutching my HRT prescription. Within a month, the hot flushes disappeared, and by three months I was noticing serious improvements to my sleep, mood, sex drive and general wellbeing. Long-term use of HRT has also been shown to improve skin elasticity and bone density, and I even think that it gave me something of my waist back. There have been studies over the years linking some types of HRT to increased risk of breast cancer, but my GP assured me that the risks are minimal for those who do not have significant risk factors in the first place.

One woman said that she will take HRT for as long as her fingers can handle the blister pack, and I totally agree with that statement. Almost half of our lifetime is lived post-menopause. We are expected to run busy households and businesses, and live normal lives for a few decades past fifty, so why do it in a mental fog while suffering from brittle bones, insomnia and depression? I am an advocate and I will shout my views from the rooftops. Any woman that does not have significant risk factors should make an appointment with her GP today and start feeling much, much better.

ENDOSPHERES

One lazy morning, while idly reading the Daily Mail (OK, I admit to the odd indulgence with trash news), I came across Endospheres. This is a machine invented in Italy which claims to lift your butt cheeks by 2cm over twelve treatments, as well as get rid of your lax skin and cellulite. It is a mechanical device with a joystick made up of 55 rotating spheres that delivers a slightly painful compression where it is needed in your body.

Not being one to shy away from new butt lifting innovations, I booked myself a session of six full-body treatments. It hurt, but not a lot! Where I have strong muscles, like the front of my legs, it hurt more. Each session was one hour long, and it worked my body, shoulders to toes. In addition to its bottom lifting claims, the treatment worked as a lymphatic drainage massage and deep tissue massage on my long-suffering left shoulder.

The results were visible and cumulative. My body was lifted, toned and visibly sculpted. I ended up doing the twelve sessions after all, and I am glad I did. A good amount of my cellulite disappeared, my bottom perked up and the chronic pain in my shoulder has greatly improved. Definitely recommended.

TANNING

A light tan softens the appearance of imperfections and gives you a natural glow. No, not the orange self-tanning or the pink glow of someone who fell asleep on the beach without any sunscreen. Nothing is more ageing for the skin than sun damage, and no tan is worth that risk. Instead, I am talking about the golden tan that builds up after a week's vacation and while slapping on 30 SPF sunscreen on a regular basis.

If there is no vacation forthcoming, there is a whole new generation of anti-ageing gradual self-tanning creams and quite a few are highly rated on Amazon. Having said that, recent research claims that they have an ingredient which actually ages the skin (DHA/erythrulose) and is especially damaging if you expose DHA-treated skin to the sun. Gradual self-tanners aren't as safe as we've been led to believe after all.

If you are concerned about protecting your skin from premature ageing, you may want to switch to a wash-off fake tan. These "tan in a bottle" products provide instant colour and are great for a night out. To get the best result, you need to go lighter on the face than the body and avoid using too much on drier areas, such as the elbows and the knees.

SMILING/TEETH WHITENING

Smiling makes you look a lot younger. As we age, our faces collapse a little and we get frown and marionette lines, which makes us look perpetually sad and a bit angry. A smile changes *everything*. Try this for yourself. Look in the mirror and give yourself a big smile. Instant facelift!

I practise my smile all the time, and you know what? It's made me a happier person. I admit that I may smile inappropriately on occasion, but the temptation to look beautiful overtakes me at random moments.

Smiling also tones the muscles around your lips, mouth and cheeks, and prevents wrinkling and sagging. More than that, smiling attracts people to you while boosting your endorphins, which reduces stress and makes you feel happier.

Of course, you don't want your smile to reveal ageing, yellowing teeth. Orthodontic treatments can run into the thousands of pounds and they will give you a bright, irresistible Hollywood smile. A more economical way to get a dazzling smile without going the whole hog is a course of teeth whitening.

Yellowing, stained teeth are the result of a life well lived, but also a sure sign of ageing. It is easy to get a quick win here and it is an area you should not neglect. I had my teeth whitened at the dentist when they were running a promotion, but I know of several friends who have done theirs at home and the result is very similar to mine.

My procedure was done in two visits. During my first visit, the dentist took an impression of my teeth. On my second visit, I was given a set of dental trays with a whitening solution to use every night. I wore those trays every night for a week. I tasted the solution while I tried to sleep, and the experience was not very pleasant. A week later, I was the proud owner a beautiful, sparkling white smile.

As a teenager, I spent two years wearing braces and keeping my mouth shut when I was around boys. I was not fitted with the barely noticeable ones that my daughter got when she turned thirteen. Mine were metal horrors that made me feel like "Jaws" from the James Bond movie, *The Spy Who Loved Me*. Much as I hated them at the time, the discomfort paid off multi-fold in subsequent years and I still have an amazing smile. These days, you can have perfect teeth at a fraction of what my parents paid for mine. The braces are invisible, and the treatment is a lot quicker.

White, straight teeth are an anti-ageing no-brainer. If your smile reveals even worse than yellowing, stained teeth, you should consider spending more time with your dentist. Your smile is your calling card. Revealing a missing tooth under a perfectly plumped-up smile will do you no favours. If you have chipped or missing teeth, you should fix those first and foremost before anything else mentioned in this book. Either that, or keep your mouth firmly shut at all times.

Finally, a word on fillings. I was not blessed with good quality teeth and I have a mouth full of fillings. Even with an NHS dentist, you can ask to pay a little extra for white fillings. I have always opted for that and I suggest you do the same. Metal in your mouth is unsightly and ageing.

Sitting in a dental chair is nobody's idea of fun but the result is totally worth it. Besides the numerous health benefits of taking care of your mouth and teeth, a beautiful smile will make you look significantly younger, healthier, more popular and *much* more attractive.

MINIMAL CHANGE WITH MASSIVE EFFORT AND HIGH COST

THREADING

Threading, also called the "lunchtime facelift" or the "bloodless facelift", became trendy a few years ago. It is a relatively painful procedure, despite the local anaesthetic. Essentially, the plastic surgeon uses a very long needle to thread a network of crisscrossed barbed wiring under your skin. This wiring dissolves after six months or so, but the body is so upset with you that it creates a net of collagen where the wire was threaded, and this creates a lifting effect which becomes visible after a few months. There is also another method, involving only one non-dissolving wire, which goes under your chin to support your sagging neck.

Once the threads are in, they become anchored under your skin with the barbs and it is impossible to get them out. Many complications have been reported because of this. Incompetent doctors have placed the threads too close to the skin surface so that the barbs are visible under the skin, or they have created unsightly bumps. You must think me crazy to have gone for this procedure, but many women did, to avoid the cost and risks of an operation. Threading can be done at the doctor's office, takes about twenty minutes and costs under £1,000.

Neck Threading

As discussed previously, I was desperate to do something about my neck, which to my eyes was saggy and unsightly. Many a woman will agree, as it is the one area that gives away your age faster than any other. Turtleneck jumpers are a staple of the over-45 age group for that reason. I have hated my neck for decades, as I was one of those people born with a turkey neck; or in my case, rather than a sagging neck it was a keen, jutting-out jaw that created an almost straight line of skin from my chin to the bottom of my neck. At least that's how I saw it, and it bothered me greatly.

Being very early in my transformation journey, I was too timid to consider plastic surgery, so when looking around for alternatives, I came across neck threading and decided to give it a go.

I was recommended a reputable doctor and a few weeks later, I found myself nervously awaiting my turn, covered in local anaesthetic cream and a plastic film on top to make it more effective. I am of a weak disposition when it comes to medical procedures, so my heart was thumping, and I kept trying to unsuccessfully meditate into a future, blissful state with no more saggy neck. I was also somewhat ambivalent because the doctor had warned me that, at my age and with the state of my neck, there was a good chance that the effect would be hardly noticeable. This procedure works better for younger people with minimal sagging.

To make a long story short, I winced as the surgeon inserted twenty barbed threads from ear to ear using a very long needle. The pain was a tolerable five, but the thought of what he was doing made it so much worse.

In my case, I saw no immediate difference from the mechanical effect, nor did I see any difference in the three months that followed. The doctor was right and my 50-year-old neck was simply too far gone for such feeble interventions to work and have a visible effect. Since then, a 40-year-old friend repeated the procedure with the same doctor; in her case, the result was visible immediately and improved even more over time. Her jawline is more defined and crisper, and she is thrilled with the result.

My recommendation regarding neck threading is to give it a miss if your neck is too far gone. To put it bluntly, there is really nothing you can do in this area that will have a visible effect, other than go under the knife – which is exactly what I did.

Belly Threading

All I can say about this procedure is "don't do it"! This really, *really* hurt and it still hurts five months later. Despite the local anaesthetic, it felt like I was being stabbed repeatedly – 25 times, to be exact – with a blunt knife. Afterwards, it felt like I was hugging a hedgehog. Five months later, it still hurts when I wear high-waisted jeans, when I bend over to tighten a shoelace, and on other occasions which are too numerous to list. In other words, I have not forgotten this procedure and maybe never will. After the total disaster of the neck threading, you may be wondering why I was stupid enough to go for more threading.

It goes like this…

When my tummy tuck fully healed, there was a small area of loose skin over my belly button which stubbornly remained. This is quite normal, and most people ignore it; or, if it is too pronounced, the doctor performs corrective surgery. In my case, it was so small that corrective surgery would have been way over the top. The doctor said that a bit of threading would fix it in a jiffy.

As mentioned previously, I did not enjoy my neck threading experience, but it was not super painful either. It was a freebie that would fix a minor problem, and that it did. What the doctor neglected to mention was that the threads used on the body are twice as thick as the neck threads, and the needle is also much wider in order to carry the thread in its hollow. He stabbed me with this needle 25 times and the pain was unbearable. It worked wonderfully and did exactly was it was meant to do. Despite that, I will never do it again and I am counting the days until the threads dissolve and stop hurting. My recommendation on this one is to run the other way as fast as you can.

MINIMAL CHANGE WITH LOW EFFORT AND POSSIBLY LOW COST

MANICURE/PEDICURE

I only have a few things to say about mani/pedis, primarily that I love having my fingernails and toenails done by a professional. It does not hurt, the results are instant, and I get to pick a colour that I like.

That said, there are real reasons to have regular treatments for your hands and feet, as they go through the ageing process in the same way as your face. Hydrating them, massaging and getting rid of dry skin gives them a youthful appearance and prevents some of the aches that come with ageing.

Hands and feet that are expertly polished, rounded and short are perceived as youthful and so is wearing rings, for some reason. Picking the right nail colour will make your hands and feet look younger instantly. A bright, orange-based red is one of the best colours to use, as it detracts attention from any age spots and wrinkles.

Blue-toned reds are not so good, as they make your veins (which get more pronounced with age) and age spots stick out like sore thumbs.

I always wear sunscreen on my hands in addition to my face and moisturise them regularly, as they tend to get very dry, especially during the winter.

SUPPLEMENTS

My daughter said the other day that our fridge looks like a pharmacy, and she is probably not exaggerating. I keep all my supplements in the fridge to keep their active ingredients from losing their potency. I recently did a clear-out and stopped using those that seem to have no effect.

I also want to preface this section by saying that anyone who eats a healthy diet gets sufficient vitamins and minerals through their regular food. The supplements I take have either been recommended by a doctor or are of a more esoteric nature, as I will describe below.

Flaxseed/Cod Liver Oil capsules: I take one of each, as the verdict is still out as to which one is better. I started taking flaxseed when I had eye surgery on the recommendation of my doctor, as it helps with eye dryness. Since then I have discovered its numerous health benefits, including healthier skin and hair, and weight loss. Flaxseed also fights cancer, helps with the symptoms of menopause and lowers your cholesterol.

When I was growing up, all good mothers forced a spoonful of cod liver oil daily into their children's reluctant mouths. Now it comes in a much more palatable capsule form and it is packed with Vitamin D, which is in short supply for those of us who live in northern climates. It promotes healthy skin, bones and joints, helps lower blood pressure and cholesterol and can even help reduce depression and anxiety. And there's more! It maintains eye health and helps repair damaged teeth, nails and hair. Not bad, eh?

Tru Niagen: This belongs in the new category of supplements that try to reverse ageing by increasing your cells' ability to make energy by raising NAD levels. This may well be mumbo jumbo to some, but there are clinical studies behind it and I am a believer based on personal experience. I will not bore you with all the science behind it; basically, we use NAD every day for basic functions, but its levels decline with age. In my case, since I started taking Tru Niagen regularly I feel a noticeable increase in energy and cognitive functions. I concentrate better and jump higher during my exercise class. I won't be giving this one up soon.

Fisetin: A relative newcomer to my fridge. As of this writing, it is completely sold out in Europe and I had to have it sent from the US. Its primary function is that it improves brain function and memory, and we all know where both of these go as we age... In studies, it was found to cause new brain growth by crossing the blood/brain barrier. There are also preliminary studies showing that Fisetin has cancer-fighting properties, but it is early days in the research. More importantly, however, a number of studies have found that it activates a gene associated with a long lifespan. So here you have it! It claims miracles and maybe it does miracles. The verdict is out.

Resveratrol: This is a powerful energy booster and is effective in reversing some of the effects of ageing, like osteoporosis and cognitive decline. It also has anti-cancer properties, and can combat obesity and increase metabolism.

MCT oil: I put a spoonful of this in my coffee every morning and it usually sends me straight to the bathroom. Unlike other fats, it goes directly to the liver where it is used as a source of energy. It improves athletes' endurance during high-intensity exercise, can stimulate weight loss and improve brain and memory function. Another good one for the arsenal.

Obviously, I cannot attest to the efficiency of any of these supplements individually. Yet, as a whole, I can say that since I started on my regimen, I jump out of bed at 6am (before my alarm has a chance to go off) and then I run around all day like the Energizer Bunny, exercising, writing my books, walking miles around London, taking care of myself and my family, and generally on the lookout for ways to expend my extra energy. Overall, I am convinced that they work well, and they are an integral part of my anti-ageing routine.

COOLSCULPTING (FAT FREEZING)

If you want to visualise something funny, think of CoolSculpting. The idea here is that your love handles (or other stubborn fat pockets) are attached to a vacuum cleaner-type device, which sucks up the fat and freezes it to kingdom come. It takes about forty minutes and is relatively painless. The first ten minutes are a bit uncomfortable, until the skin becomes numb. When they unhook you at the end of the treatment and your body begins to defrost is no picnic, either. But overall, it is not one of the bad procedures, and it works.

Unfortunately, you have to wait a few months to see any results, but when they come, they are quite transformative. It takes time for your body to gradually expel the dead fat cells. Having deep tissue massage or an Endospheres treatment on top of the frozen area can speed up the process by breaking down the dead fat.

In my case, after two treatments, two months apart, my love handles melted away. I know of two friends who had similar experiences. My all-knowing doctor says that the treatment works for most people but not everyone, and when it works, it works very well. Prices vary wildly, but you can get one treatment on Groupon for little more than £100. The machine is the same everywhere, so I see no reason to pay more.

CoolSculpting, as the name suggests, is not effective for overall fat loss. It is to be used for stubborn fat pockets such as love handles, belly fat, arms and – try not to laugh at the mental image – man boobs.

HAIR SERUMS/OLAPLEX

There are literally thousands of hair treatments, masks, serums and treatments. Over the years I have tried many, with varying degrees of success. I suspect that the results depend a great deal on your individual hair typo. Howovor, thoro ic ono that stands out above all the others, especially for bleached and dyed hair that breaks easily. I am speaking about Olaplex.

When it first came out, I hunted all over London to find the few salons that offered it. Now, it is available widely and I encourage you to try it. It is the only treatment that actually links broken bonds in the hair, before, during and after any chemical treatment. Olaplex revolutionised the hair industry.

Not to get too scientific here, but Olaplex works at the molecular level, finding broken bonds and restoring them. No other treatment can restore broken bonds – in that regard, it is unique. It is applied at a salon, and there is a third step (maintenance) that can be done at home. Since I started using it, my hair is shiny, has more volume, and all the damaged ends look healthy and bouncy. A real winner!

FACIALS/GLYCOPEEL

I have had precisely ten facials in my 55 years. Some felt better than others, mostly depending on the therapist rather than the process. Many women claim that they get some sort of "glow" from a facial. The industry wants you to believe that a facial will combat wrinkles, regenerate your skin and get rid of all your blemishes. I am afraid that this "glow" and its associated benefits has eluded me.

Scientific dermatological research fully supports my experience. Any benefit that you may observe is temporary. It is simply not possible for any creams to reach the deeper skin layers in this manner. The skin is a fantastic barrier and slapping on the goop has primarily psychological (rather than actual) benefits.

I also tried the much-vaunted Glycopeel using glycolic acid, which claims to stimulate skin cell turnover and thus repair the ravages of time. If it made any difference, it was so minuscule that it went completely unnoticed. Do your own research before you spend your money. You may get more enjoyment splurging on a massage than your next spa visit.

CREAMS AND SERUMS

The subject of creams and serums is endless, and everyone has their own favourite creams, serums and moisturisers. I don't believe I have much to contribute here, other than to say that in my view, almost every cream or serum I have used is as good as any other. I have paid from as little as £6 to as much as £145 and I have noticed no difference whatsoever.

There is a recent school of thought claiming that moisturising does more harm than good. Skin gets addicted to artificial moisture and becomes "lazy", thus not supplying natural hydration. My view is that if my skin needs extra hydration, it will tell me. If it feels dry, I moisturise; otherwise, I don't. The main thing I use religiously is a high-SPF sunscreen and a cleanser. If at any time my skin feels dry, I use any of the many half-opened tubs of cream littering my makeup table. I have made a pact with myself to not buy another cream or serum until all the half-open ones are gone, and they will probably expire long before this happens.

I had a chat on the subject of face creams with my surgeon, who generally looks fresh as a daisy, and his view is that the only effective creams have a good concentration of retinol and vitamin A. Having said that, I did use the Environ range (only available in beauty salons and doctor's offices) religiously for a year. They have a method where you start with a tub of low retinol concentration and work your way through five tubs of progressively higher doses. I may as well have used Tesco's own range, for all the difference it made.

I have a similar opinion on face masks. I don't think they have much to offer and if they do, I have not noticed any before-and-after difference on my skin. I use the ones I have left to entertain my children, pretending to be the Creature from the Black Lagoon or a space alien. They work brilliantly for that.

The skin on your hands takes a lot of beating on a daily basis and soon gives away your age. If the serum that you use on your face is too expensive to use on your hands, the supermarket Aldi has a highly praised range of creams and serums for under £7 ("Lacura" brand). I use the night cream and serum on my hands, and any other parts of my body that are dry and prone to age discoloration.

LASER TREATMENT

For Discolorations

This treatment is designed to get rid of any discolorations and age spots decorating your otherwise flawless face. It can be done in two to three sessions and it is quite effective. The pain level is moderate, and the treatment is quick. It feels a bit like someone flicking a rubber band on your face while surprising you with a super bright red light. Your eyes are shut and hidden behind black goggles, yet the red light finds its way through undisturbed. I am not sure if I was bothered more by the light or by the flicking, but after three passes of the laser, I was happy to be done.

This treatment cannot be done in the summer, as you need to protect your face for a few weeks following the session, and you cannot have a suntan when you have it done. I did mine during the dark, grey days of the English autumn, and not a ray of sunshine got anywhere near me for almost a full month. In fact, if you live in the UK you can probably have it done most months of the year...

In the days that follow, you have a very slight peeling of the lasered areas and most of the discoloration goes with the layer that peels off. If the marks are not completely gone, you go back for another round of flicking and red lights. It is effective and not too expensive. I give it the thumbs up.

For Hair Removal

When I was in my twenties, it was more than sufficient to run a razor blade across my armpits, bikini line and legs below the knee and hit the beach for a hot date. The more sophisticated amongst us would go to the beauty salon at the start of the summer to get their legs and bikini line waxed, in a treatment that can only be described as pure torture. In fact, it was so painful that I recall only one attempt, which ended up in only half a leg done before I bolted.

How times have changed! These days, women and men alike are supposed to groom, wax or laser all their body hair within an inch of its life. Young people will simply not tolerate a bush down below. In fact, one of the first signs of infidelity was when my ex took a razor to his privates…but this is really another story for another book.

Speaking of down below, there are a few options, starting with the extremely well-groomed "bush", to the landing strip or the Hollywood option (going bald). A very sophisticated industry comes to the rescue to tackle this hairy issue. New technologies in wax and lasers have made extreme pain a thing of the past. Still, getting rid of hair in some areas is no picnic.

After a few sessions of very uncomfortable waxing, I opted for the more permanent solution of laser treatment. I have the ideal combination of light skin contrasting with dark hair, which is what a laser prefers. It is harder for dark skinned people to laser without burning, but I know there is a new type of laser than can solve this problem by using a dual-wavelength, depending on the skin colour.

Older people have advantages when it comes to hair removal. Because metabolism is slower and hormones are fewer, hair growth is also limited. This means that what goes may never come back and if it does, it will be sparser. There is, of course, a fly in the ointment… Grey hairs cannot be targeted by the laser, so do not wait too long if you are planning to go ahead with this treatment

For an effective treatment, I was instructed to shave the day before and avoid tanning booths and tanning in general for a few weeks prior. At the salon, I was given a pair of dark glasses and told to strip naked. The therapist uses a joystick-like device to zap little clumps of hair away. I am not too hairy, so I didn't bother with arms or upper legs, but I had a few pesky chin hairs (inherited from my mother) which I was very happy to kill once and for all. The pain level varied by area, with underarms being the least bothersome and the "mound" down below being the most sensitive. I was given an icepack and told to stop being a baby.

The whole thing took fifteen minutes, but several treatments are required. Each session gets rid of 15% of hair permanently and everything falls off within a few days of the procedure. I needed twelve sessions and I will need to return for top-ups once a year, to zap any errant hairs that appear.

There are incredibly good deals for this treatment on Groupon, as every clinic seems to have acquired a laser and the clientele has multiplied. If you want to keep up with the times and get rid of the weekly hassle of shaving or the exquisite pain of waxing, I recommend this treatment.

MAKEUP AND MAKEUP CLASSES

The advent of YouTube and Instagram took the makeup world by storm. From age thirteen, my daughters had more bottles, tubes and palettes than I would acquire in a lifetime and knew how to use them with the panache of a seasoned Hollywood makeup artist. They are able to practise their contouring, highlighting and other mysterious skills on the bus to school. I would not have bothered, as I am lazy in that department...but I really love the outcome of their efforts, and felt the urge to dazzle with my new Instagram account.

To my credit, I read a lot of articles and even sat in front of my computer with a selection of makeup items and an instructional video, but the result was less than satisfying. There are thousands of videos catering to the very young, but few and far between for women of a certain age.

I went searching for professional instruction and managed to land an excellent deal for a one-on-one, three-hour makeup class at the Makeup London Academy. A very patient Aussie worked with me to pick the shades and colours best suited to my face. She taught me contouring, eyeliner placement, how to use an eyeshadow pallet, how to blend properly, etc.

She was absolutely wonderful and even wrote it all out for me to take home. She did one eye, I did the other, she took everything off and watched me do it from scratch on my own. She took pictures before and after, and finally sent me home with a small parting gift. I never knew you could do so much with makeup, especially when it comes to lifting all your features using highlighting and eye makeup. When she was done, the girl who stared back from the mirror was much younger than the one who had walked in three hours prior.

Totally worth it and highly recommended for anyone who is stuck in the 80s with their makeup technique. Here are a few tips for us older ladies:

- We have cracks and crevices. A tinted primer will even everything out.

- Avoid heavy foundations with total coverage. They are made for acne-prone teenage girls or Instagram queens. On older skin, they highlight the wrinkles and look awful. CC creams work well during the day; use a foundation with a bit more coverage for a flawless evening look.

- A good concealer is your friend. You can use it to cover such thing as pigmentation, thread veins and dark under-eye circles.

- As we age, we lose colour in our face. Use a non-glittery blush to add a touch of colour to your cheeks; a crème blush works better than powder.

- Avoid all powders, as they make wrinkles stick out.

- An expertly applied eyeliner can lift your whole face.

- Do not use matte lipsticks or blue/gold/etc. eyeshadows, as they are terribly ageing.

- Use a brightly coloured gloss lipstick and avoid pale colours that are similar to your skin colour. They do not work well for older faces.

- Don't forget your black mascara to give your eyes a defined look, and use a brow pencil to fill in your brows where they are sparse.

SOME CONSIDERATIONS

What if I Don't Have the Money?

If your budget is zero or very low, here are the things you can do that have minimal cost and will still make a significant change:

> ➢ Exercise regularly, including doing plenty of resistance training and the 8 Minute Abs

> ➢ Keep your weight at the low end of the healthy BMI guidelines

> ➢ Always wear sunscreen

> ➢ Grow your hair to below shoulder length, condition it regularly, trim the ends and keep it as close to your natural colour as possible

> ➢ Take care of your nails and toes with regular at-home mani/pedis

> ➢ Go through your wardrobe and do a proper clear-out

> ➢ Watch YouTube tutorials to update your makeup skills; expertly applied makeup can take a decade off your face
> ➢ Use a pharmacy-bought kit to whiten your teeth
> ➢ Smile a lot!

I'm Too Afraid of Pain…

I can sympathise. I too am very afraid of pain and, unfortunately, there is quite a bit involved in beauty. Surprisingly, the least pain I experienced was during surgery, which is the bloodiest and most invasive of procedures. There is the aspect of the general anaesthesia, but I also seemed to need no pain relief in recovery.

I ranked all the procedures based on the level of pain experienced, most painful first:

Threading Tummy (with local anaesthetic) – PAIN LEVEL 10

HIFU (High Frequency Ultrasound) – PAIN LEVEL 9

Permanent Makeup: Eyeliner/Lips (with local anaesthetic) – PAIN LEVEL 7

Plastic surgery: Tummy tuck/Liposuction (with general anaesthetic) – PAIN LEVEL 5

Plastic surgery: Breast augmentation (with general anaesthetic) – PAIN LEVEL 4

Plastic surgery: Neck (with general anaesthetic) – PAIN LEVEL 4

Threading Neck (with local anaesthetic) – PAIN LEVEL 4

Permanent Makeup: Eyebrows (with local anaesthetic) – PAIN LEVEL 4

Needling (with local anaesthetic) – PAIN LEVEL 3

Laser For Discolorations – PAIN LEVEL 3

Laser Hair Removal (hurts a lot LESS than waxing) – PAIN LEVEL 3

Laser Eye Surgery – PAIN LEVEL 2

Botox (with local anaesthetic) – PAIN LEVEL 2

Fillers (with local anaesthetic) – PAIN LEVEL 2

CoolSculpting – PAIN LEVEL 1

Hair Extensions – PAIN LEVEL 1

Endospheres – PAIN LEVEL 1

Teeth Whitening (at the dentist) – PAIN LEVEL 0

Eyelash Extensions – PAIN LEVEL 0

Facials/Glycopeel – PAIN LEVEL 0

Smiling – PAIN LEVEL 0

You may notice that the most painful procedure was also the least useful, in my case. HIFU was very good, but I am not sure I would do it again. Permanent makeup just looks amazing and is totally worth the pain. Plastic surgery was more inconvenient than painful and the "gross-out" factor is quite high. Most procedures actually fall under the 4-or-below pain level, which is very manageable for most people.

Of course, pain is subjective. To give you an idea of my pain levels: I found labour pain to be the maximum 10;

falling and scraping my knee is a 5; breaking my little toe, a 6; having my tooth filled, a 3; a root canal is level 6; and lastly, a deep tissue massage is pain level 2.

As for my happiness level every morning when I wake up and look in the mirror, that is a 10. You be the judge.

My Family/Husband/Kids Do Not Want Me to Change…

I suspect that any resistance would primarily concern surgery – your family is worried about the risks and possibly the cost. The best way to approach this is to explain to your family why you want to change, and how much this transformation will mean to you. Also, with a keen eye on the family finances, you should have a plan for covering the cost. Perhaps you can take on a part-time job, or forfeit a vacation or new outfit. It is important to demonstrate to your family that you are willing to make sacrifices to pay for the surgery.

If you feel insecure and unhappy about how your body looks after multiple pregnancies and breastfeeding, you need to let them know. You may also not be ready to hang up your gloves and call it quits on the beauty front, or you may have a particular part of your body that has always bothered you. Where is the harm in that? Whatever your reasons, your family *will* see benefits from a happier you.

Plastic surgery, especially in older women, is known to improve emotional wellbeing. A recent study showed that breast augmentation and reduction were most uniformly associated with positive emotional outcomes, with women reporting that they felt greater social confidence and self-esteem. The same study also showed that self-perceptions of physical attractiveness relate strongly and positively to happiness. Another study revealed a wide range of benefits, including improvements in anxiety, social phobia, depression, body dysmorphia, goal attainment, life satisfaction, mental and physical health, self-efficacy and self-esteem. Nothing to sneeze at!

I am not saying that such drastic and invasive transformations are for everyone. However, if you feel you will benefit from a procedure and have the means to do it, your family should support you and not stand in your way.

I Am in My Late Thirties, Should I Be Doing Anything Now?

I don't recall needing anything done when I was in my late thirties. My advice to you is to exercise regularly, use sunscreen and enjoy these beautiful years, where you know enough to be confident and you are still considered young.

If you have issues with your complexion, you may want to complete a course of needling, maybe Botox to smooth out any wrinkles. Can I also suggest permanent makeup? It made my life so much easier. I wish I had done it when I was younger, thinking about it. If you are blind as a bat like I was, I strongly suggest laser eye surgery. It makes such a difference not having to faff around with contact lenses.

The beauty industry will try to convince you that you need all sorts of things, even in your thirties. When you reach 50, you will look back on those years and realise that you needed nothing (or very little).

I'm Too Busy...

Most of the procedures I described can be done during your lunch hour and have minimal downtime. If you decide to go ahead with plastic surgery, you will obviously need to schedule time off from work and the family. I organised mine around holidays with the kids.

I would go ahead a few days before, have the surgery, and arrange for the kids to fly a few days after. We would spend a relaxing week together in some quiet location before returning to our daily lives. This was my way of doing it, obviously you need to look at your own circumstances and see how it will work best for you. My view is that if it matters to you, you will find the time and a way.

I Don't Want People to Know Because They Will Think That I Am Vain...

If your doctor is skilled, all people will notice is that you are looking great. Some procedures will be obvious. There is no way to hide larger, perkier breasts and they don't sprout overnight at 50! Same problem with hair extensions. Most everything else will only be noticed by your nearest and dearest, if you chose to keep it private. As for me, I decided early on that I was going to be open with everyone about everything. In fact, I am even publishing my beauty adventures in this book so that you can all benefit from my experiences.

IN CONCLUSION

All these procedures are costly, and some are quite painful, but the results are spectacular. I look at pictures from ten years ago and much prefer the way I look today. This may sound ludicrous, given the many thousands of pounds that I have spent so far to get me where I am…but in the long run, I have saved a fortune in facials, lipstick, eyeliner, foundation, expensive creams and moisturisers, and my makeup table looks positively streamlined. I don't need to wax anymore, and I can often leave the house with zero makeup, still looking glam.

More importantly, I like the image in the mirror. The older woman that kept showing up has been banished for now, and this is very satisfying. When I was younger, I thought about my weight. Not just occasionally; all the time. Now, I think about my wrinkles all the time, and how to keep them off my face. I read voraciously every article that comes out about innovations in the anti-ageing arena, and I am not shy to try new things.

To make one thing clear: I *don't* want to live forever. Far from it. I just want to look good and be healthy for as long as I walk this Earth.

Is This All There Is?

This book would not be complete without discussing the internal transformation, as well as the external. It is easy to limit yourself to working on your *outer* self, as it is the one that is the most bothersome (at least initially). For me, seeing such a disconnect between what I saw in the mirror and the image of the girl in my head was truly disturbing. I would look down and seriously try to imagine what I would look like in a coffin.

OK, I am being a little dramatic, but you get the picture. Not a happy bunny. Fast-forward a few years and – several thousand pounds later – I can look in the mirror and smile at my reflection, quite happy with the result.

Yet, I was not fulfilled. Something significant was certainly missing. I was still unsettled, I felt that the years were rushing by and I was just waiting…waiting for what, was a bit unclear. The carefree beauty in the mirror was not carefree, but full of the responsibilities of middle age. The outside had not magically changed the inside, even though it had relieved much of the angst.

I needed the *oomph* to start something new. Sure, I had plenty of ideas but I kept hitting the immovable argument of: "Why? What's the point? I really can't be bothered…"

What I needed was nothing that plastic surgery or hair extensions could achieve. I needed the starry eyes of someone who has not seen it all, and risen and fallen with the passing decades; one who had been betrayed and seen death engulf those close to her. But where to buy this? Which doctor can perform this sort of procedure?

Rebuilding the Inside

Here I will give you an important secret to happiness, so pay close attention because I worked hard to discover it!

Reaching middle age can be incredibly liberating. The shackles of convention can be shaken, and the world is your oyster to be discovered. The problem, of course, is that we don't realise that. Blindly, we keep putting one foot in front of the other, leaving all adventure for some unspecified future date. For some very strange reason, we are programmed to think and act as if our time is unlimited. All our actions point to this false belief. We strain under the heavy weight of our mostly self-imposed endless responsibilities, yet we keep doing the same thing over and over until the very end.

To break the cycle, I started with a week's retreat. Any retreat that forces you to examine your life choices will do. The idea is that being in a new environment, away from the daily drudgery, you will be more objective and dispassionate when considering your options and your future life. This worked very well for me and it works for most people who try it. Everyone goes home with an armful of notes and a catalogue of life-altering decisions.

I also started looking at my "responsibilities" in a different way. Every single one was questioned. Every "must do", "can't change", "impossible to do any other way" that had guided my life to that point was re-examined to see if it were true. This was an incredible process that made my burdens lighter with every revelation.

It became quite clear that the possibility of a new chapter in life was just as important as a new face or body for happiness. The saying goes that the young have life ahead of them. What this really means is that they have *possibilities*. A mature person is thought to have narrowed those possibilities into concrete choices that frame their life path until the end. I believe that this is where the problem lies. You cannot feel young and hopeful if all is already decided and predetermined.

I set a goal to push my comfort zone in some way at least once a week and expand, rather than shrink, my world. Take a new route, introduce myself to someone new, make a new friend, agree to do something frivolous and unexpected, write a book... My close friends span several decades in terms of age and live on four different continents. When a new technology appears on the horizon, I put my hand up to try it out. I feel totally liberated from responsibilities and anxieties.

But the most important revelation has come with the concrete and absolute knowledge that I can and will do what I want – as long as it doesn't hurt anyone else – and that the opinions of others matter very little, compared to how I think about myself.

It is a funny way to end a book about anti-ageing treatments, but I need to shout it out. I am finally fully comfortable in my skin! (…but I will not be giving up the Botox any time soon.)

ALEXANDRA FILIA

"I love helping women find happiness. This is my passion. Admittedly, I went through several careers and had many adventures before I finally settled down long enough to write The Good Breakup and Love is a Game. On a small sailboat, I explored the world for 7 years, married twice and founded and sold a successful business in the City of London.

What I am most proud of, however, is the many women I have helped in their search for their soulmate. In one year alone, I was maid of honour in 14 weddings and in my book, I will teach you all the techniques you need to come out of a breakup whole, excited about life and ready to find your own fairy tale romance."

Alexandra Filia was born and raised in Athens, Greece before moving to New York to complete her studies. She worked as a stockbroker, banker and in professional publishing before selling everything and moving onto a boat. She sailed the world, writing about her adventures in a series of articles published in a cruising magazine. When she arrived in London on her boat "Nikia", she founded and sold an award-winning business while raising two toddlers.

She has married and divorced twice and her expert advice has helped several people get over their heartbreak, leave a toxic relationship behind and find the love of their dreams. She and her partner share their home in London with her two amazing teenage daughters.

Alexandra has published three books in the Dream Series: "Love Is A Game: A Marriage Proposal in 90 Days", "The Good Breakup: Take a Deep Breath and Remember Who You Really Are" and "Forever Young: An Anti-Ageing Guide for the Terrified".

www.loveisagame.net

Continue the discussion at the *Love is a Game Facebook Group* (women only) at:
http://bit.ly/joinloveisagamegroup

Also by Alexandra Filia

Love Is A Game: A marriage proposal in 90 days

The Good Breakup: Take a Deep Breath and Remember Who You Really Are

Printed in Great Britain
by Amazon

33875400R00061